Tropical Saltwater Aquariums

SEYMOUR SIMON

Illustrated by Karl Stuecklen

THE VIKING PRESS NEW YORK

Tropical Saltwater Aquariums

HOW TO SET THEM UP AND KEEP THEM GOING

FOR LINDA ZUCKERMAN

MY GOOD FRIEND AND EDITOR

First Edition

Text Copyright © Seymour Simon, 1976
Illustrations Copyright © Viking Penguin Inc., 1976
All rights reserved
First published in 1976 by The Viking Press
625 Madison Avenue, New York, N.Y. 10022
Published simultaneously in Canada by
The Macmillan Company of Canada Limited
Printed in U.S.A.

1 2 3 4 5 80 79 78 77 76
Library of Congress Cataloging in Publication Data
Simon, Seymour.   Tropical saltwater aquariums:
how to set them up and keep them going
Bibliography: p.   Includes index.
Summary: Discusses setting up and maintaining a saltwater
aquarium including selection and care of the inhabitants.
1. Marine aquariums—Juvenile literature. 2. Tropical fishes—
Juvenile literature. [1. Marine aquariums. 2. Tropical fishes]
I. Stuecklen, Karl.   II. Title.   SF457.1.S56   639'.34   76–14447
ISBN 0-670-73191-9

Contents

INTRODUCTION:
The World of a Coral Reef

In the warm waters of tropical and semitropical seas, there are many jungles, made not of plants but of living stone. The living stone is coral; the underwater jungle is a coral reef.

A coral reef is the natural home of most of the tropical fishes and other animals we keep in a marine aquarium. In nature it is a strange and beautiful community of living things. Living corals are a riot of many colors: scarlet, yellow, violet, green, brown, pink, and white. The fishes and other animals that move among the coral are just as spectacular, with brilliant colors and patterns and strange shapes.

A stony coral animal can live only in very special

surroundings. The water must remain warm all year around: between 68° and 82° F. (20°–28° C.) The water must be fairly clean and be in constant motion. Each coral needs enough food, oxygen, and light to continue its life processes. These conditions exist only in fairly shallow waters that occupy a broad belt around the world on both sides of the equator.

Coral reefs are found in the Caribbean Sea, along the coast of Brazil, in the Red Sea, along the Great Barrier Reef off the coast of Australia, in the Indian Ocean, and in the warm Pacific. All in all, coral reefs cover an area of about two million square miles.

Each tiny living coral looks like a stony cup surrounded by a veil of transparent, colorful jellylike material. A ring of tiny wriggling tentacles around the edge of the cup reaches out for food in the constantly moving waters in which the coral lives. New coral cups grow from the sides of older ones, forming large coral colonies.

Coral colonies are called by the names of the objects they resemble. Among these are the rounded masses of brain coral, the large branching staghorn coral, finger coral, lettuce coral, and organ pipe coral. Stony coral colonies are often covered by soft corals such as red, yellow, and purple sea fans and sea rods. A piece of branching staghorn coral weighing one pound may consist of as many as forty thousand tiny coral animals.

Most coral reefs contain masses of both living coral colonies and the stony skeletons of dying or dead coral. Living reefs are growing all the time. Small coral islands and great coral reefs have been constructed over many years by the tiny animal. Along the northeast coast of Australia is the largest mass of coral in the world: the Great Barrier Reef. It is about one thousand two hundred miles long and one hundred miles wide.

The coral survives through a strange partnership with plants. Within the soft tissues of a coral animal are many microscopic green plants. The plants need sunlight to grow and produce food. The growing edges of a coral reef are high enough for sunlight to filter down through the water and yet not so high that the coral would reach above the water and dry out.

The coral animals that house the tiny plants receive two bonuses: the surplus food that the plants manufacture and the extra oxygen that the plants give off during this process. On the other hand, the plants use the carbon dioxide and mineral salts that are given off by the coral animals. Both plants and animals benefit from their relationship.

In and around the coral live great numbers of small animals. Worms burrow into the coral or build tubes attached to the coral. The coral protects the worms' bodies from fishes and other passing enemies. From the ends of their tubes the worms' highly colored, flowerlike heads are visible, gently waving in the water. The shadow of a diver's hand or of a passing fish makes the worms instantly withdraw into their tubes.

Sea stars, snails, shrimps, crabs, flatworms, and sea slugs crawl in and among the coral rocks. Some feed on the coral; some feed on each other. Peculiar looking animals called sea squirts grow in bright orange and purple masses around the sea fans and sea rods. Spiny black sea urchins shelter in the shade of a coral overhang. (It's a good idea to avoid stepping on a sea urchin. Their sharp pointy spines are poison-tipped.)

Deeper down in the reef are a great number of fishes. Many are brightly colored with weird shapes and patterns. Parrot fish, with mouths that look like a parrot's beak, bite off small chunks of coral to get at the plants growing on the rock. Small, gaily colored damsels defend their little home territories. An orange and white striped clownfish swims unharmed within the poisonous tentacles of an anemone. (See page 46.) Magnificent butterfly fishes and angelfishes display their colors as they move among the stony columns of the reef.

An octopus glides along the bottom on its eight legs. It blows away a layer of sand and quickly engulfs a hiding crab. Schools of grunts and snappers swim by, looking for food and avoiding becoming food themselves. Larger, solitary fishes such as the grouper or the moray eel feed upon the unwary animals that venture too close to their hiding places.

Keeping the colorful animals of a coral reef in a home aquarium can be a fascinating and enjoyable experience. Each time you look at the animals' incredible colors and shapes and watch their sometimes strange behavior, you will realize how much there is to learn and to think about in the natural environment you have set up and maintained. It is a hobby that will keep you interested for a long, long time.

A coral reef is filled with life because its living conditions are so favorable to life. The reef provides protection and food for a host of animals. The ocean currents around a reef are in constant motion, always refreshing and renewing the waters in the reef. The temperatures and chemical makeup of the water stay fairly constant. Any changes in the environment of a coral reef are very small and last for only a short time.

For these reasons the animals of a reef have never developed the ability to adjust to a variety of different surroundings. Unfavorable conditions in nature simply do not exist for them. And therein lies the difficulty in keeping coral fishes in a home aquarium. A marine aquarium is not a miniature ocean. It must be treated differently in order for the fishes to survive.

Fishes and other animals of a coral reef are very sensitive to changes in their surroundings. Chemical changes occur in the water of an aquarium that do not take place in the ocean. Yet despite the differences between the natural environment of a coral reef and the artificial environment of an aquarium, it is still possible for you to keep marine animals for long periods of time. In fact, once you understand how and what to do, keeping a saltwater aquarium is no more difficult than keeping a fresh-water aquarium. We hope this book will help show you the way.

·1·
Seawater in Your Aquarium

Have you ever gone swimming in the ocean or watched a film showing life in the sea? The water may look as clear as the water from your kitchen faucet. Yet unlike the water that you drink, seawater is full of unseen life.

You can't see the living things in a glassful of seawater because they are too small. Yet even the most transparent seawater contains thousands of microscopic one-celled animals and plants. These tiny living things are called *plankton* by scientists. The word comes from a Greek word which means "drifting" or "wandering."

Both animals and plants make up the sea's plankton. Most of the tiny plants are called *diatoms*. They come in all different shapes. Under a microscope you can see that many have long needles or spines sticking out from their bodies. Diatoms are used as food by the small animals of the plankton.

Animal plankton also come in many kinds and shapes. Most are just a bit larger than the tiny plants they eat. Some are still larger and can be seen by your unaided eye. They look like little specks swimming through the water.

If you were to collect seawater to use in an aquarium, you would not be able to avoid taking in large numbers of animal and plant plankton. The water would start to change immediately upon being placed in an aquarium. The tiny animal plankton would eat the plants and each other. They would use up the oxygen in the water and give off carbon dioxide. Many would die quickly. Their remains would decay.

Soon the water would become unfit for other, larger forms of ocean life such as fish. In the spring, when plankton is most abundant in the ocean, the seawater you collected might begin to smell bad only a few hours after it has been collected.

There are other reasons why natural seawater may not be the best choice for a home aquarium. The water may be polluted by chemicals or traces of garbage. It may contain bacteria or other harmful organisms. Water close

Diatoms and Plankton, greatly magnified.
(relative sizes not to scale)

to the shore is often the worst kind to use in an aquarium because it is the most polluted.

Yet you can use natural seawater in your aquarium if you follow certain precautions. The water should be collected as far offshore as possible. Sand and silt particles should be filtered out by pouring the water through several thicknesses of nylon material. The water should then be stored in tightly sealed plastic containers for a month. During this time the water can be kept at room temperature.

After this the water will probably be fit for use. Pour off the water from the top of the containers so that any silt will remain at the bottom. Use only plastic or glass containers for seawater. Metal buckets will release chemicals that are poisonous to sea life.

Does all this sound too complicated for you? There is a much simpler way to set up a saltwater aquarium. You can use synthetic or manmade seawater. Synthetic seawater is easy to get, simple to use, and free of most of the problems involved with using natural seawater.

Real seawater is a very complex substance. It contains traces of almost every natural element known to science. Synthetic seawater resembles it only slightly, yet it works just as well in an aquarium. With synthetic seawater even people who live far inland can set up and maintain saltwater aquariums in their home.

The first synthetic seawater was made in the 1850s and contained a few simple salts. It could be used for only the hardiest of sea animals. But today's synthetic mixes are a much different story. They may contain thirty or forty different compounds. These are the substances that are necessary for the normal growth and life processes of sea animals.

There are many different brands of synthetic marine salts. They can be purchased through the mail (see the advertisements in aquarium periodicals) or from a local saltwater aquarium dealer. Most marine salts come packaged in preweighed plastic bags. The contents of the bag are mixed with a specified amount of ordinary tap water. Each brand of marine salt will have its own directions for mixing on the package.

Use all the salt in the package when you mix up a batch of seawater. The packages usually come in sizes suitable for five, ten, or twenty-five gallons. Be sure to measure the right amount of water.

You can mix the salts and the water right in the aquarium before it is set up, but that is not the best way. The ideal way would be to use a large plastic container such as a plastic garbage pail. Naturally, the garbage pail should be clean and not used again for anything else. The pail should have a tight-fitting lid. Place the pail on top of several bricks or a sturdy low table. This will enable you to siphon out the water into smaller containers so that it can be carried to the aquarium.

Check the volume of the can by pouring in known amounts of water. Use a crayon or strip of plastic tape to mark off five-gallon divisions. This will help you in future mixings. Most synthetic seawaters are cloudy when they are first mixed. Stir them well with a wooden or plastic stick. (Remember: do not let any metals come in contact with the water.) You can transfer the seawater to your aquarium when it turns clear in a day or two.

The saltiness of seawater can be measured by an instrument called a hydrometer. A hydrometer floats in water. If you have ever tried floating in both salt and fresh water, you know how much easier it is to float in the salt water. In the same way, the more salt that is dissolved in the water, the higher the hydrometer floats.

The thin top of the hydrometer is marked off in lines and numbers. The numbers refer to a measure called *specific gravity*. The specific gravity is a ratio of the weight of a sample of seawater to the weight of an equal volume of fresh water. Pure fresh water has a specific gravity of 1.000. Normal seawater has a specific gravity of 1.025.

To check the saltiness of your seawater, float a hy-

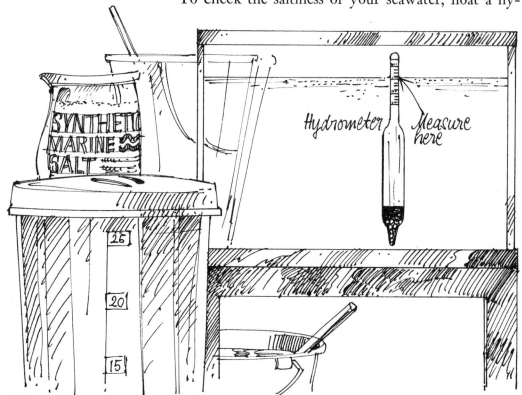

drometer in the water. Wait for it to stop bobbing up and down. Read the number at the place on the thin part of the instrument that is right at the water level. The best reading for the animals living in an aquarium seems to be about 1.023, somewhat below that of natural seawater. In Chapter 3, we'll explain how you can adjust for this reading.

Another important property of seawater is its pH value. The pH value of any solution is a measure of its acidity or its alkalinity. A pH of 7 is neutral—neither acid nor alkaline. Numbers under 7 down to 1 show that the solution is acid. Numbers above 7 up to 14 show that the solution is alkaline. Seawater in nature is about 8.0 to 8.3, slightly alkaline.

If an aquarium is set up and maintained properly, the pH will usually remain within a safe range (7.5 to 8.5) for the fishes. Over a long period of time pH sometimes tends to drop. You can purchase an inexpensive kit to measure the pH in your aquarium, but it probably isn't necessary. Monthly or biweekly water changes (see page 76) will usually keep the pH in the reasonable range.

·2·

What You Will Need

All of the materials presented in this section can be purchased by mail from various aquarium-supply companies around the country. But all or most of the materials can be purchased also from local pet stores that have a section devoted to tropical fishes.

THE AQUARIUM TANK

There are different kinds of tanks in use in many homes today. Some have frames made of stainless steel or other metals. Some are made of plastics. All these tanks are perfectly fine for fresh-water fishes. But they are not as good for saltwater. The metals may rust and poison

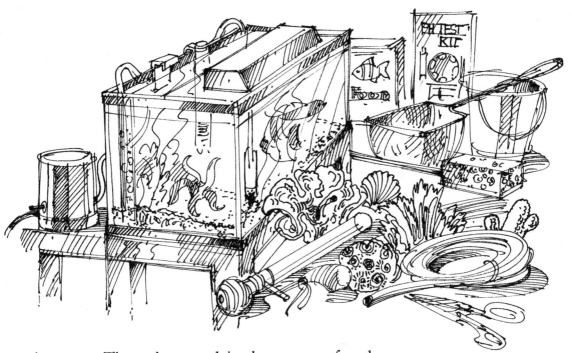

the water. The sealants used in these types of tanks to prevent leaks may also be dangerous to marine life. Plastic also scratches easily and becomes unsightly.

The only type of tank to consider buying for salt-water aquariums is an all-glass one. The modern glass aquarium tank is made of five pieces of glass: the four sides and the bottom. The glass is held together with a silicone sealant. The sealant stays flexible and waterproof for an indefinite time. Many all-glass tanks have top and bottom rims of a plastic trim.

As all-glass tanks have become more popular, their prices have come down. A standard shape all-glass tank should cost less than one dollar per gallon. Tanks come in two basic styles: low and high. The low tank is longer and has a greater surface and bottom area than a high tank of the same capacity. It is the better of the two because surface and bottom area are more important in an aquarium than water depth, as you will see.

The larger the marine tank you set up, the greater your chances of successfully keeping the fishes alive. Small tanks are more apt to become overcrowded and have their water go bad. On the other hand, large tanks are more expensive to buy and run, and more difficult to set up and maintain. For these reasons the best size for a beginning saltwater enthusiast is no smaller than twenty gallons and no larger than forty gallons.

At the same time that you buy the tank, you should consider buying a stand for it. Sea water is very heavy; it weighs about eight and one-half pounds per gallon. A twenty-gallon tank when filled with water, sand, and coral will weigh close to two hundred pounds. It needs a good sturdy stand. A wrought iron stand made especially for aquariums should cost less than half the price of the tank.

FILTERS

In order for the water in your aquarium to last for any length of time without fouling, you *must* use a sub-sand or undergravel filter. This is a plastic plate perforated with holes or slits that fits snugly across the entire bottom of the aquarium. A plastic pipe, or airlift, fits into holes in the corners of the plate. The filter is covered with gravel, but allows water to circulate underneath. An undergravel filter needs an air pump to power it.

This kind of filter will keep the water clear and process some of the harmful waste products fishes give off. Without an undergravel filter, the gravel would become a stagnant area for the buildup of pollution products. Eventually these pollutants would kill the animals in the aquarium.

There are other kinds of filters available for aquariums. These filters are set up outside the tank. They use substances such as spun polyester fiber, sponge, and/or charcoal to filter particles from the water. An outside filter may be used in *addition* to an undergravel filter but not *instead* of it.

AIR PUMPS

An air pump furnishes a flow of air which constantly moves the water through the gravel. The animals in your aquarium depend upon the water movement; without it they would quickly die. You should be able to buy a good quality pump for ten to fifteen dollars in any aquarium-supply store.

There are two different kinds of pumps usually available: vibrator or piston. Either would be suitable, but a vibrator pump is generally less trouble to maintain. Along with the pump, purchase ten or twelve feet of plastic airline tubing and a gang valve with at least three outlets. The tubing and valves are needed to connect this pump to the filter.

HEATERS AND THERMOMETERS

Since you are going to keep tropical fishes, you must maintain the water at a constant temperature even during cold weather. An electric immersion heater has a glass tube

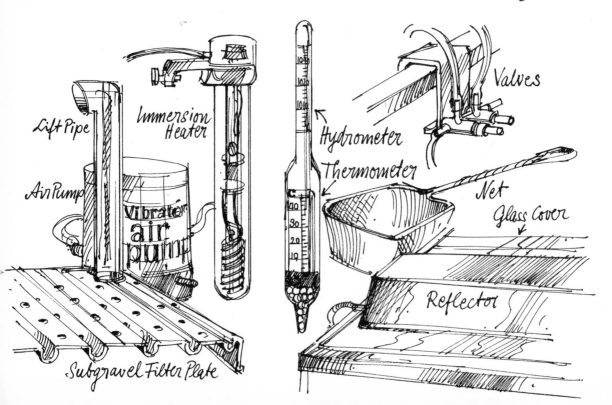

Lift Pipe

Air Pump

Immersion Heater

Vibrator air pump

Hydrometer

Thermometer

Valves

Net

Glass Cover

Reflector

Subgravel Filter Plate

which goes into the water and a plastic top which hangs over the side of the tank. You can set the temperature at which it will maintain the water by means of a dial on top. A glass or plastic thermometer kept submerged in the tank will help you keep tabs on the water temperature.

Heaters are rated by their wattage. In the colder sections of the country, five watts per gallon is about right. Warmer areas could use less than that. Ask the dealer from whom you buy your equipment what he recommends.

REFLECTORS

It is not a good idea to set up an aquarium in a sunny spot near a window. The water may overheat and harm the fishes. But you do need light to observe your fishes easily. The answer is a reflector or hood which contains incandescent light bulbs or fluorescent tubes. Either kind is suitable. A fluorescent tube is more expensive to buy but uses less electricity.

Be sure to purchase a reflector that will fit the size of your tank. For a saltwater tank, the best kinds are made of plastic or stainless steel. Cheaper materials will rust and foul the water. At the same time, it is a good idea to cover the tank beneath the reflector with a sheet of glass. This will reduce evaporation and protect the reflector as well. Many aquarium-supply houses sell a hinged glass cover just for this purpose.

GRAVEL

The kind of gravel you use is important to the success of your saltwater aquarium. The gravel must contain the mineral calcium. Calcium will help to keep the correct chemical balance of the water. Most aquarium supply companies sell dolomite, limestone, or crushed oyster shell for this purpose. The gravel grains should be rough and sharp, not smooth and rounded. The sharp edges make a better filter. Grain size should be a bit less than one-quarter of an inch.

Purchase enough gravel to make a layer three inches deep over the undergravel filter. A depth of gravel less than three inches will reduce the effectiveness of the filter. It is *not* a good idea to use beach sand in your aquarium. The grains are usually too small and will pack together and prevent water from circulating. The sand may also contain animal parts which might decay and pollute the water.

CORAL, ROCKS, AND SHELLS

Coral is particularly useful in a saltwater tank. It offers hiding places for the more timid kinds of fishes and helps to keep the water chemistry correct. Coral can be purchased from an aquarium dealer or in specialty stores.

Before coral can be used in an aquarium it must be

cleaned and washed thoroughly. Place the coral in a plastic container and cover it with fresh water to which a cupful of laundry bleach has been added. Allow the coral to soak for several weeks. Empty the container and wash the coral carefully under running water. It must be rinsed of any trace of the bleach. Even the slightest amount of bleach will poison a saltwater tank.

Shells can be treated in the same fashion as coral. It is very important that spiral shells, which have large inside chambers, be cleaned thoroughly. One good way to make sure that there is no decaying material in a shell is to make a hole in the back through which water can flow.

The best kinds of rocks to use in a marine aquarium are limestone or calcite rocks. These should be cleaned too. Do not use any rocks that may contain metals or other substances which will dissolve in the water. If you have enough coral, you can omit using any rocks at all.

OTHER EQUIPMENT

You will need a net to catch fishes in your aquarium when it is set up. You do not need anything else to start a saltwater aquarium. Equipment such as protein skimmers, ozonizers, ultraviolet tubes, and the like are for use by advanced aquarists and are not necessary for success.

SUMMING UP

You will need these things:

1. An all-glass aquarium tank of from twenty- to 40-gallon capacity. A stand to match.
2. An undergravel filter to fit.
3. An air pump, along with plastic air tubing and valves.
4. A heater and a thermometer.
5. Enough dolomite or limestone gravel to make a three-inch layer over the entire bottom of the tank.
6. A light reflector.
7. Prepackaged marine aquarium salts, enough for your tank and some extra for emergencies.
8. A hydrometer to test the saltiness of the water.
9. Coral for decoration.
10. Plastic pails for mixing and carrying water.
11. A net for catching fishes.

A NOTE ABOUT COSTS

Many aquarium stores will sell a complete outfit of a tank, air pump, filter, heater, etc. for less than the total price of each item. This could be a good deal as long as you get what you want. The price for a complete twenty-gallon saltwater set up would probably range upward from fifty dollars.

·3·

Setting Up

Decide beforehand where you want to set up your aquarium. You will not be able to move your aquarium around after it is full of water, so wherever you place the tank will be a more or less permanent spot. Try to locate the aquarium so that it is free from cold drafts from a window or a door and away from direct sunlight. Also make sure there are no expensive pieces of furniture nearby; they are almost certain to get wet.

Set the stand in place on the floor. The legs may not be even and the stand may tip back and forth slightly. Don't worry. The weight of a filled tank will force the legs down and make the stand very steady.

With the aid of a friend set the tank on the stand. It

should just fit, with the edges of the tank and the stand almost even all around. Using a plastic bucket, fill the tank half full of tap water and allow it to stand for half an hour. Now check the outside of the tank for leaks. If there are any leaks, return the tank to your dealer. Don't try to fix it yourself. (The chances of getting an all-glass aquarium that leaks are very, very slight.)

It is a good idea to wash your hands at this point. Use only a little soap. Be sure all the soap is rinsed off your hands before you place them in the aquarium. If the aquarium is dusty or has dirt in it, use a *new* sponge to clean the inside and outside. Keep the sponge for use only in the aquarium.

Dip or siphon out all the water you can. You can use a small plastic container for dipping water. Remember that everything placed in the aquarium must be without the slightest trace of soap or any chemicals on it. After almost all the water has been removed, have your friend help you to tip the tank and pour out the last bit. Don't try to lift a glass tank with even a gallon of water in it, because you could easily crack the glass. Replace the tank on the stand after all the water has been removed.

Rinse the undergravel filter thoroughly under running water. Assemble the filter according to the directions on the package (it's a very easy assembly job) and place it in the tank. It should just cover the entire bottom of the tank.

The dolomite or calcite gravel that you purchase in a pet store will be dusty and must be washed. Wash about five pounds of gravel at a time. Place the gravel in a clean plastic bucket and hold it under running tap water. Keep stirring the gravel around with your hands. After a few minutes, the water running over the sides of the bucket should look clear. Pour out all the water in the bucket, using your hand to prevent the gravel from coming out. Place the gravel into the tank on top of the filter.

Wash all the remaining gravel in the same way. When all the gravel is in the tank, smooth it evenly over the filter with your hands. Some people like to have the gravel slope slightly towards the front of the tank. This is all right but not really necessary. You should have at least three inches of gravel over every part of the filter.

If you are also using an outside filter, set it up at this time following the directions on the package. If the filter contains charcoal, it must be washed before use. The charcoal is also very dusty and will leave a black ring in the aquarium if it is not first rinsed.

Set the air pump in the spot that you are going to keep it. Attach one end of the plastic tubing to the outlet of the pump. Run the other end up to the top of the tank where the gang valve is to be hung. Cut the plastic tubing with a scissors or sharp knife. Attach the end to the side stem of the valve. Hang the gang valve in the back top of the tank.

Cut and attach other pieces of tubing from each of the filter air tubes to the top stems on the gang valve. Use the diagram that comes with the filter or the diagram on page 27 to see how this looks when it is set up.

Now you can add the seawater that you previously mixed. (See pages 10–11.) When filling the tank, set a plastic container on the bottom and pour the water into it. This will break the force of the water and prevent the gravel from being pushed around. It will also help to prevent splashing water all over you and the floor. Fill the tank to about two or three inches from the top. Remove the plastic container and smooth over the gravel when you finish.

Allow the water to stand quietly for fifteen minutes. Then place the hydrometer in the water. After it stops bobbing up and down, take a reading. If the reading is higher than 1.023, you must add some *fresh water* to bring down the saltiness. Add about one quart of fresh water at a time. Be sure you mix the fresh water with the seawater thoroughly before you take another reading.

After the water is adjusted to the right saltiness, you can plug in the air pump. The air flow from the pump will start the undergravel filter bubbling. Use the valves to adjust the flow of air so that both of the lifts are bub-

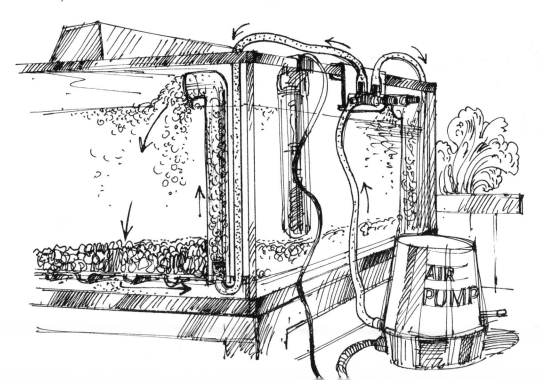

bling about the same. The bubbles should be coming up fairly rapidly.

Set the heater in place in the back of the tank. Read the instructions that come with it so that you can adjust the temperature correctly. The indicator light in the heater will tell you when it is on. Hang a thermometer from the side of the tank opposite to the heater. Try to adjust the heater to make the temperature in the tank about 75° F. (24° C.).

Check the thermometer after several hours to see if the temperature is right. If you want it warmer, turn the thermostat on the heater so that the light comes on again. If you want it colder, turn the thermostat the other way so that the light goes off.

If you want to use coral or rocks as decorations add them at this time. (Make sure you clean them according to the instructions on pages 20–21.) The coral will look better if you place the larger pieces around the sides and toward the back of the tank. Allow the front center of the tank to be empty so that it will become the main swimming area.

Set the glass cover on the tank and place the reflector on top of it. Check the temperature and the saltiness of the water the next day to see if any adjustment is needed. Allow the water in the tank to stand for at least twenty-four hours before you add any animals.

·4·

The First Weeks

The first few weeks after a marine aquarium is set up can be the most difficult time. The gravel in the aquarium has not yet been conditioned to handle the chemicals produced by the fishes. Only the hardiest of marine fishes can survive in a new aquarium. Yet a beginner is tempted to purchase the most colorful (and expensive) fishes that he sees in the tanks of a dealer. Often these fishes are the most expensive because they are the most delicate.

Resist the temptation to buy colorful butterflies and angel fish until the aquarium has been set up for at least one month—even longer is better. There are many kinds of fishes that are hardy and inexpensive. Many of them

are also quite lovely. Start with any of the ones mentioned in Chapter 7.

There is a good reason to be careful. Pollution in an aquarium comes from two sources. One is the living animals themselves. Marine animals give off chemicals such as ammonia and other kinds of nitrogen compounds. Uneaten food and dead animals and plants are the other source of pollution. Harmful substances will gradually build up in the aquarium, finally poisoning the animals.

In a home aquarium only an undergravel filter can keep this from happening. The undergravel filter is a biological or living filter. You can't see it work, and unless you have all kinds of testing chemicals, you can't even measure its effects. Yet without this kind of filter, keeping marine animals alive for any length of time would be impossible.

Biological filtering comes about as a result of the action of helpful microscopic bacteria living on the gravel along the bottom of the tank. These bacteria have come to the gravel in different ways: from the air, from the animals in the tank, from the foods you feed them, even from your hands as you put them in the water. As the aquarium ages, the helpful bacteria increase their numbers enormously.

Finally the gravel is teeming with bacteria. It is then that the aquarium can really function well. This process usually takes a few weeks, so during these first weeks keep only a few hardy fish in the tank.

You can speed up the time it takes for the gravel to become conditioned in several ways. One of the best ways is to take a handful of gravel from an old, established marine aquarium and add it to yours. Perhaps the dealer from whom you bought your supplies will allow you to take a handful of gravel from one of the tanks he keeps.

The old gravel is probably full of bacteria that you need. They will quickly multiply and spread through the gravel in your tank. This method can result in cutting in half the time it takes for your gravel to become conditioned.

If you can't get any gravel from an established marine aquarium, there is another method that you can use. Add your fish one at a time, a week apart. This will give the gravel a chance to adjust to each new increase in chemicals in the water. This method is a good idea anyway, since it is the safest for the animals.

The bacteria in the gravel need oxygen to live, just like the fishes and other animals in the tank. Because of this the undergravel filter should be kept going all the time. Of course you can shut down the air pump for short periods to service it, but in no case should it be shut off for longer than an hour or two.

Even though the bacteria in your aquarium can take care of some pollution, you have to help. Try to keep the pollution from building up. Almost as serious as shutting off the air supply is keeping too many fishes and other animals in the tank, overfeeding them, and not removing uneaten and decaying food promptly. If the pollution increases too rapidly, the bacteria will simply not be able to cope with it, and the fishes will die.

How many fishes are too many? This depends upon a number of different factors. The old rule of thumb for fresh-water aquariums is one inch of fish for each gallon of water. But this doesn't work for marine aquariums. For one thing, it doesn't take into account the area of the gravel which is doing the filtering.

Here is the best way to figure out how many fishes you can safely keep in your aquarium. Find the surface area of the gravel in square feet by multiplying the width by the length of the tank. Assuming a depth of at least three inches of gravel, for each square foot of surface area, you can keep three inches of fish.

For example, suppose your aquarium is 12 inches wide and 30 inches long. Multiplying 1 foot (12 inches) by 2.5 feet (30 inches), you get an area of 2.5 square feet. At 3 inches of fishes per square foot, 3 multiplied by 2.5 is equal to 7.5 inches of fishes.

The 7.5 inches of fishes can be divided in many ways.

You can have seven or eight fishes, each one-inch long. You can have one seven-inch or eight-inch long fish. You can have three two-inch long fishes and two one-inch long fishes. The length of a fish should not include its tail fin. How you want to divide the number is up to you. But remember: the number of fishes your tank can hold is for a conditioned tank. Start building up to that number slowly.

· 5 ·

Introducing New Animals to Your Aquarium

The first secret to success in keeping marine fishes alive and healthy is to choose healthy ones right from the start. The fishes that you see in a dealer's tanks are the survivors of a very difficult journey. Some have been caught by nets and others by being drugged. The fishes have been placed in buckets, banged around, overheated or chilled, rarely fed, and shipped by land and air over great distances. It is a wonder that any of them are still alive!

The fishes or other animals that you buy are in need of your close attention from the moment you take them out of the dealer's tank. Everything in your aquarium at

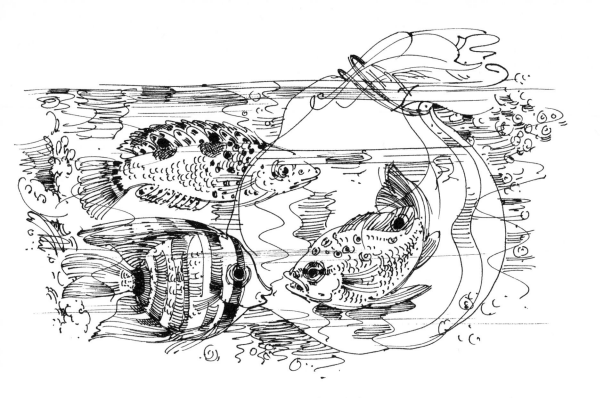

home should be in readiness. Don't stop off and do some more shopping. Take the fishes right home and follow the directions in this chapter for placing them in your tank.

Here are some tips on picking healthy fishes from your dealer. The first thing to observe is a fish's behavior. A healthy fish should be swimming easily and without peculiar movements. Does it get very frightened when you look in the tank and dash around crazily? Reject such a fish. (Of course, you should *never* tap on a tank. The noise will frighten most fishes.)

A healthy fish has clear, bright colors. Faded colors

could be the result of many things, from a skin disease to being kept too long in the dark. Since you can't be sure what is the real cause, don't buy a fish with faded colors.

As you check the color of a fish, look carefully for cuts or other damage to its fins and scales. Sometimes these will heal without any difficulty. But sometimes they will become badly infected and the fish will die. Don't take chances. Reject any fish with visible damage to its body.

Finally, ask the dealer to drop some food into the tank for the fish to eat. A healthy fish will go after food immediately. If the fish is not interested and doesn't eat in a dealer's tank, it may not eat in your home tank either. Don't buy a noneater.

A fish should be caught from a tank by using a plastic bag, not a net. A net can scrape scales off a fish and can easily injure its eyes. The plastic bag should be filled with the water in the tank in which the fish was kept. A rubber band is used to tie the plastic bag closed. You can place the plastic bag in a paper bag to carry it home. Some dealers may insist on using a net to catch a fish. Be sure to recheck the fish for any injury after a the dealer places it in a plastic bag.

When you get your fish home, make sure you don't remove it from the paper bag into a bright light. Some fishes will go into shock at a sudden burst of light. For the same reason, keep the aquarium lights off while the transfer is going on.

Allow the plastic bag to float in the aquarium for *one hour*. This will allow the temperature of the water in the bag to become the same as the temperature of the aquarium water. This is very important. Fish can easily go into shock and die if they are transferred very suddenly into water of a different temperature.

After an hour, check the water temperature in the plastic bag with a thermometer. If it is the same as the water temperature in the aquarium you can proceed. Add a little (about one cup) of the tank water to the contents of the bag. Keep adding a little tank water every fifteen minutes for a total of one hour. This will gradually get the fish used to any differences in the chemical content of the water.

At the end of the hour, gently tip the bag sideways, and let the fish swim out. Don't just pour the bag of water with the fish in it into the aquarium. Remember, you are trying to make each step in the transfer as gentle as possible for the fish.

Keep the lights in the aquarium off for the rest of the day. After a few hours, if the fish is swimming around easily in the aquarium, try giving it a light feeding. (See Chapter 6 on foods and feeding.) Feed the fish lightly for the first few days.

·6·

Foods and Feeding

There is one rule in feeding that is more important than any other. *Don't overfeed.* You may think that you are doing the fishes in your aquarium a favor by giving them lots of food all at once, but instead you may kill them. Excess food will not be eaten. It will remain in the tank, decay, and pollute the water.

Too much food at one time is particularly bad in the first few weeks or months after the tank has been set up. The bacteria in the gravel are not yet able to turn large amounts of waste matter into harmless chemicals. It is far better to feed your fishes a little food often than a lot of food at one time. A small meal two or three times a day is ideal.

Feed enough food so that all of it is eaten in two or three minutes. Any food left over should be promptly taken out of the aquarium. It's important to watch the fishes as they eat. You can see if all the fishes are getting food rather than just one or two of the most aggressive. You can also see if there is any excess food left in the tank.

If you feed your fishes at the same times each day, you'll see that they will become very active as you approach the tank. They have become conditioned to being fed at your approach. They will come to the surface at the point where food is introduced, even before the food hits the water.

There are many different kinds of food that are suitable for saltwater tropicals. One good kind is the flesh of fish such as flounder, haddock, or halibut. Any fish flesh is good as long as it is not too oily. Keep the fish in the freezer until feeding time. Cut off a small chunk and let it thaw out. Carefully scrape or cut the fish into chunks small enough to be swallowed at a single gulp.

Place a few pieces in the tank at a time. When they are all eaten place a few more pieces in the tank. In this way you can see when the fishes seem to lose interest in the food, and you can prevent serious overfeeding.

Shrimp is another good food. Raw shrimp is better than cooked shrimp. Keep the shrimp frozen until just before use. Take out just the amount you need and let it thaw. Remove the head, legs, and shell of the shrimp. Cut the flesh into small pieces and feed as before.

A different kind of shrimp that you can buy in most aquarium-supply stores is frozen brine shrimp. These are not for human consumption. Always buy the frozen *adult* brine shrimp. Frozen *newly hatched* brine shrimp, which also are usually for sale, are too small for most aquarium animals.

Brine shrimp in frozen blocks come packaged in plastic bags of various sizes. Keep the bag in the freezer until just before feeding time. Break off a small piece of the frozen block and place it in a clean glass with some water. The shrimp will thaw and separate in a few minutes. Drain off the top of the water. You can use a medicine dropper to pick up a number of shrimp at a time and place them in the aquarium.

Some aquarium-supply stores also sell containers of living brine shrimp. These can be fed by netting them and transferring the net into the tank. The fishes seem to love the moving brine shrimp. They will clean them out in no time. The only problem is that living brine shrimp are more expensive than the frozen blocks. But you might like to give living brine shrimp to your fishes as a treat once in a while.

Some stores that specialize in marine tropicals carry other kinds of frozen foods. These include clams, squid, and even plants such as kelp. They come packaged in the same kinds of plastic bags as brine shrimp. Feed them to your fishes in the same way as you would any frozen food.

There are also many kinds of dry, prepared foods available in aquarium stores. The best of these are the ones that come in flakes. You can feed these to your fish by crumbling a pinch of the flakes between your fingers and dropping it into the tank. The pieces will float on the surface of the water. After a few minutes, you can easily remove the excess flakes with a net.

Don't use the packaged dry foods that are made up mostly of insect parts. They usually will not be eaten and are difficult to find and remove once they are in the tank.

Don't worry about feeding your fishes if you go away for a weekend or even longer. Fishes are cold-blooded animals and can get along without being fed for surprising lengths of time. Of course, if you are going to be away for a week or longer, arrange for someone to come in and feed your animals. Be sure to give them exact directions on what and how much to feed.

Other than brine shrimp, there are several live foods that you can use. These include daphnia (a small freshwater relative of brine shrimp), tubifex worms (small red-

dish worms sold in aquarium-supply houses), and small hard-shelled animals found in shallow seawater such as sandhoppers.

Still another good food for larger marine fishes are the young of fresh-water livebearing fishes such as guppies, platies, and swordtails. Feeding live baby fishes to larger fishes may not seem quite right to you. But remember that in nature fish is the natural food of fish. There is an old saying that goes something like this: "Big fish eat little fish, and little fish eat littler fish, and so on, ad infinitum."

SUMMING UP

1. Don't overfeed.
2. Feed small amounts at a time. Wait until all the food is eaten before placing any more into the tank.
3. Small meals two or three times a day are preferable to one large meal.
4. Remove any uneaten food promptly.
5. Vary the kinds of foods you use.
6. Don't worry if the fishes are not fed for a day or two. They are better off without food than being overfed by an inexperienced person.

·7·
Fishes for the Beginner

An ideal saltwater tropical fish for a beginner would be colorful, lively, not too large, hardy, and inexpensive. Fortunately there are many fishes that fill these requirements. It makes sense to learn how to keep a healthy, thriving marine aquarium by starting with one of the fishes discussed in this chapter.

A NOTE ON SCIENTIFIC NAMES

The same fish may be known by many different names in different parts of the country. And in countries with other languages, the difference is even greater. Some aquarium dealers even invent descriptive names for fishes in their tanks. How is anyone to know that a "lionfish" is the same as a "turkeyfish?" Or that three fishes, all called "blue devils," are really different from each other?

The answer is to use a common system of names that is agreed to by scientists the world over. All living things are grouped according to a system begun by the Swedish scientist of the eighteenth century, Carl Linnaeus. Scientists decide which animals are most alike in body structure and in the working of their body organs. They use these likenesses to group animals together.

In this book, each fish is identified by both its *genus* and its *species*. Since Linnaeus wrote in the scientific language of the day, Latin, all scientific names are still written in that language.

As an example, here is the scientific classification for the common clownfish.

Kingdom	Animal
Phylum	Chordata
Subphylum	Vertebrata (vertebrates)
Superclass	Pisces (fishes)
Class	Osteichthyes (bony fishes)
Family	Pomacentridae (Spiny gill covers)
Genus	*Amphiprion* (rough edges on sides of head)
Species	*percula* (little perch)
Scientific name:	*Amphiprion percula*

In every country of the world, *Amphiprion percula* is the same white-striped, orange fish that you will commonly call a clownfish.

DAMSELFISHES

The damsels are just about the perfect group of fishes for a marine aquarium. They are almost always available for fairly low prices in aquarium-supply stores. They are among the hardiest and liveliest of all the saltwater tropicals. They are small fishes, most often one or two inches long. And many of them are brilliantly colored.

The clownfishes, or anemone fishes, are the most famous and probably the most beautiful of the damsels. These fishes can swim among the tentacles of sea anemones without being harmed. Sea anemones are dangerous because they will release poisonous stinging cells from their tentacles when they come into contact with the body of a fish.

For a long time no one knew how clownfish protected themselves from the stings of anemones. But now there is proof that the clowns coat themselves with mucus from the anemone. An anemone will not release its stingers into anything covered with its own mucus. For example, a piece of sponge that has been rubbed over the skin of a clown will not be stung, but an untreated piece of sponge will be stung quickly.

A clownfish must follow a certain pattern of behavior before it can live in safety with an anemone. You can actually see this happen in an aquarium. (You must provide the right kind of anemone for this to happen, however. See Chapter 9, page 71.)

When the clownfish and the anemone are first placed together in a tank, the clown approaches with a great deal of caution. The clown hovers just beyond reach of the anemone's tentacles. It seems to nibble at the end of the outer tentacle. The anemone stings the fish, but only slightly because the fish only touches the tip of the tentacle.

Gradually the clown works its way into the anemone. It is stung less and less. The anemone seems to become quieter and its tentacles relax. Finally the clown is able to dive into the center of the anemone without being stung at all. The whole process has taken a few hours.

Now the clownfish will flee into the tentacles of the anemone whenever the clown senses danger. Since other fishes will give an anemone a wide berth, the clownfish is safe from their attacks as long as it stays within the tentacles.

Does the anemone benefit from this relationship? Probably not very much. It is true that some food may spill over from a clown's meals, but it seems that the main benefit goes to the fish. In fact it has been found that anemones live longer in tanks where they are kept by themselves rather than with clownfishes. This should not prevent you from keeping a clownfish with an anemone —they can be one of the most fascinating parts of all aquariums.

The common clownfish, or orange anemone fish (*Amphiprion percula*), is the one most often seen in dealers' tanks and is the least expensive. Its background color is orange with three white bands across, each band edged in black. Clownfishes are collected throughout the tropical Pacific and Indian oceans, and the Red Sea.

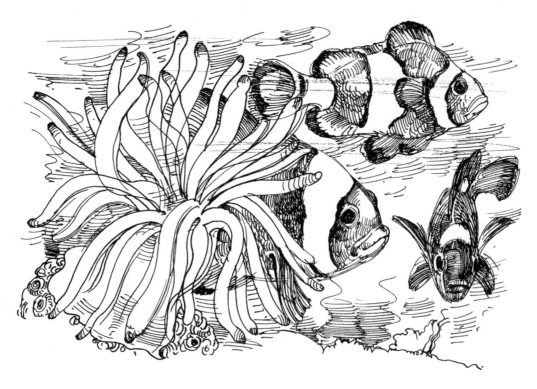

The tomato clown (*Amphiprion ephippium*) has a body color that may range from bright red to brownish red. Usually a white stripe runs over the head. This fish is one of the hardiest of all marine tropicals and is ideal for a beginner. Only one of these should be kept in a tank for they are very aggressive toward others of their kind.

The black clown (*Amphiprion sebae*) has a black or dark brown body. When young it has three white stripes, but the third stripe fades as the fish matures. A black clown's tail and pectoral fins are yellow; the other fins are black. This is an aggressive fish and should be kept without others of its own kind. It is a good fish for beginners.

There are a number of other clownfishes that you may see in dealer's tanks. These include the pink skunk clown (*Amphiprion perideraion*), the chocolate clown (*Amphiprion xanthurus*), and the saddleback clown (*Amphiprion polymnus*). All are hardy fishes that are easy to keep. They usually will do better if you keep only one of each kind.

Another easy-to-keep group of damselfishes are the different *Dascyllus* species. In nature they live in schools around the coral reefs. When some danger threatens, they dive all together into openings in the coral. Sometimes a young *Dascyllus* will live in association with a sea anemone like the clownfish. But in a tank, adults will never do this. *Dascyllus* and clownfish make an easily heard clicking noise with their mouths.

Finely chopped up bits of fish and shrimp are ideal food for all damsels. Most will also eat flake foods. While mated pairs of damsels have spawned in many aquariums, it is best for a beginner not to try to keep more than one of each kind of *Dascyllus* in an aquarium. This is not too important when they are young, but as adults, *Dascyllus* damsels become very aggressive. In fact they will often attack your finger if you place it in the aquarium.

The tri-mac or domino damselfish (*Dascyllus tri-maculatus*) is one of the commonest, least expensive, and hardiest fish around. Its body is black with a white dot on each side and one on its head. Young tri-macs are deeper black than the adults.

The *tri-mac* is belligerent toward almost any other fish in the tank. It will select a corner or a piece of coral as its home territory, and any fish that comes too close will be immediately chased away. At the same time it grunts and clicks away angrily. In nature it is found in the same ocean areas as the clownfishes.

The humbug damselfish (*Dascyllus aruanus*) is similar to the *tri-mac* in that it is hardy, plentiful, and very aggressive. Its white body is marked with three black bands. Humbugs can live in a wide range of temperatures, sur-

vive large amounts of pollution, and eat almost anything. This is another excellent fish for a beginner.

Among other hardy damselfishes for beginners are the blue devil (*Pomacentrus coeruleus*), the sergeant major (*Abudefduf saxtilis*), the yellowtail blue devil (*Chromis xanthurus*), and the green devil (*Chromis coeruleus*). The name "devil" is an unfortunate one; these fishes are no more devilish than any others.

GOBIES

Gobies form a large family of saltwater fishes. They range in size from under one inch to about two feet. Most gobies live in shallow, coastal waters along the sandy bottom or in coral reefs. They need hiding places which they defend against other fishes.

Gobies are funny fishes to watch. They roll their eyes from side to side in a very comical fashion. They usually hop from spot to spot along the bottom of a tank rather than swim. At least two of the smaller gobies can be kept by beginners.

The neon goby (*Elacatinus oceanops*) is a slender fish with a bright blue band running the length of its body. In nature neon gobies live in mated pairs. Several gobies can live in an aquarium together so long as there is enough food and space. They are bottom dwellers and have small mouths, so be sure that they get food in small enough pieces to eat. A goby's maximum size is about three inches. The neon goby is found mainly along the coast of Florida.

The varying goby (*Gobiodon rivulatus*) is less frequently seen in dealers' tanks. Its color varies from brown to red to pink. They are best kept with other small fish because they do not compete well for food. They reach a length of two inches. The varying goby is found in the Red Sea and in the Indian and Pacific oceans.

SEA BASSES AND GROUPERS

These are hardy and interesting fishes, but they have several drawbacks. A sea bass or a grouper will grow to a large size and will eat any smaller fishes in the tank that will fit into its enormous mouth. A sea bass is also a good digger and will disturb the gravel in the tank. If you keep any other fish with a sea bass, make sure it is equal in size.

The leopard fish or panther fish (*Chromileptis altivelis*) is a fancy-looking fish with blue-black polka dots on a grayish background. It paddles along in a strange fashion but can move very quickly when startled. It will eat almost anything and is very hardy. Young panther fishes seem to get along perfectly well with damsels. The panther needs some good hiding places in the aquarium. When it becomes familiar with its surroundings it swims about slowly on the lookout for food. The panther is found in many areas of the Pacific and Indian oceans.

The golden-striped grouper (*Grammistes sexlineatus*) is safe to keep with other fishes when it is about two inches long. But be careful when the grouper grows larger: it may decide to make a meal of a smaller tank-mate. It is found throughout the Pacific and Indian oceans.

There are other groupers that can be kept in a tank,

but most grow too large very quickly. If you like the way they look, try setting up a tank and keeping just one grouper in it. In a short time, the grouper will come to the surface whenever you come near the tank. Actually it's not being friendly; it's just on the lookout for food.

BRACKISH WATER FISHES

There are a few very hardy fishes that can live in either salt or fresh water. These fishes can easily be kept in a marine aquarium. They can stand almost any kind of

water, will eat anything that you place in the tank, and are lively and quick moving. They are also relatively inexpensive. Their only drawback is that some kinds may frighten less active tankmates.

The spotted scat (*Scatophagus argus*) is either greenish or reddish. Both color varieties belong to the same species. Scats are silver-dollar-shaped fishes that live in shallow inshore waters but only rarely in coral reefs. They are hardy and will eat any plant or animal foods that you provide.

The mono or Malayan angel (*Monodactylus argentus*) is a silvery, flat-bodied fish with yellowish fins. Monos should be kept in small schools of three or four fishes. They are inexpensive fish and very resistant to diseases. Monos should have adequate hiding places because other fishes tend to bully them. They make a good choice for beginners.

SUMMING UP

Choose one of the fishes listed in this chapter as the first in your aquarium. Each week you can add one more fish until your aquarium is up to its maximum carrying capacity. Make sure the fishes you choose are about the same size. It's best to buy a young fish rather than a more mature one. Young fish are more adaptable to changing conditions and are also less expensive.

· 8 ·

Fishes for the Advanced Aquarium Keeper

Some aquarium fishes are so spectacularly patterned and colored that they look unreal. Often they are large (for aquarium fishes) and spectacularly expensive too. After you have been keeping some of the smaller and easier fishes for many months, you may be tempted to try your hand at keeping an angelfish, a butterfly fish, or a triggerfish. You should be very experienced before you even try one of these. Here are some things you should know before you buy one and bring it home.

ANGELFISHES

The angelfishes along with the butterflies may be the most beautiful fishes that you will ever see. They are also

the most difficult to keep. They are very prone to infection and disease. Many of them will not eat in an aquarium. Some become very frightened in a new aquarium, go into shock, and die. If you are still tempted to try to keep one, be sure you select a healthy fish from the dealer's tanks (see pages 35–36).

Angelfishes often have pancake-shaped bodies that are thicker than those of the butterflies. Sometimes the colors of young angels and adult angels of the same species are so different that they look like different kinds of fishes. The change to adult colors usually comes when a fish is about four inches in length.

Angelfishes will defend a territory against others of their own kind. So it is not a good idea to keep two together in the same tank. However, two different species that do not resemble each other may be kept together.

Feeding angelfishes is a problem: Most will accept only small bits of food. But other fast-moving fishes in the same tank will often snatch food away from them. In nature angelfishes eat plant as well as animal life. In an aquarium they will browse on algae growing on the sides of the tank or on the coral. If there is not enough of an algae growth in your tank, try supplementing an angel's diet with bits of lettuce or kelp. (See page 41.)

The French angelfish (*Pomacanthus paru*) and the gray angelfish (*Pomacanthus arcuatus*) look almost exactly alike when they are young. Each is black with four yellow bars across its body. Adult French angels are black with yellow-edged scales. Adult gray angels are gray with a black dot on each scale. Young angels are hardier in a home aquarium than the adults. Both French and gray angels are found in the Carribbean Sea and tropical parts of the Atlantic Ocean.

The emperor angelfish (*pomacanthus imperator*) is thought by many to be the most spectacular fish of all. Young emperors are blue with ringlike white stripes. Adults have a yellow head with a black bar through the eyes. Their bodies are blue or blue-green with many yellow lines running from head to tail. When you first place an emperor angel in your aquarium, start it on a diet of live food. Later after the emperor has begun to eat regularly, you can alternate live food with frozen food. The emperor angel is found in the Red Sea and in tropical areas of the Pacific and Indian oceans.

The Koran angelfish (*Pomacanthus semicirculatus*) is more often seen in dealers' tanks than the emperor. It is also easier to keep. There is a great deal of color variation in this species. Young fish are blue with white, curving bands across their bodies, somewhat similar to young emperors. Adults have a greenish-yellow body with black spots and dark long fins. Koran angels are found in the same areas as emperor angels.

The rock beauty (*Holacanthus tricolor*) is yellow when young with a large black spot ringed with blue. As the fish grows, its color changes to orange-yellow, and the spot grows to cover most of its body. Rather difficult to keep free of infection, the rock beauty needs plant material in its diet to stay healthy. It is found in the Caribbean and tropical areas of the Atlantic.

Other angelfishes that you might see in a dealer's tanks are the coral beauty (*Centropyge bispinosus*) the cherubfish (*Centropyge argi*), and the queen angelfish (*Angelichthys ciliaris*). The first two are easier to keep than many other angels.

BUTTERFLY FISHES

Butterflies are among the most sensitive of all marine tropicals. They are picky eaters, often going on hunger strikes for no apparent reason. Even if they do eat well in an aquarium, they still seem to lose weight. In nature butterflies are constantly on the hunt for small animals in and among the coral. Most will also eat algae.

Butterflies should be fed with small pieces of food that fit their mouths. Also make sure that aggressive tankmates do not chase them away from their food. Most butterflies should be kept in tanks without others of their

own species. Ask your aquarium dealer which fishes he keeps with a particular kind of butterfly so that you can use the information as a guide for your own aquarium.

The wimplefish (*Heniochus acuminatus*) is an exception to the rule that butterflies are poor eaters. It will eat almost anything, including flake foods. But the wimplefish is still very sensitive to the quality of the water. It is also about the lowest priced of the butterflies.

The wimplefish is very pretty, with black stripes against a silver-white background. As a young fish it sometimes swims up to much larger fishes and begins picking at their gills and sides. It is acting as a "cleanerfish," a fish that eats the tiny animals that infect the skin of many kinds of fishes. An adult wimplefish can grow to eight inches in length, but you can often purchase young ones that are about two inches across. In nature the wimplefish is found in many coral reefs throughout the Pacific.

The long-nosed butterfly (*Chelmon rostratus*) uses its long, pointy mouth to get in among the coral after small food animals. This fish is also a picky eater, but it does like live food such as brine shrimp. Make sure that you buy a specimen only after you have seen it eat in a dealer's tank. Copper-colored bands against a white background make the long-nose a beautiful fish for any tank. It is found in the Indian and Pacific oceans.

The four-eye butterfly (*Chaetodon capistratus*) is found in the Caribbean and tropical Atlantic. Somewhat easier to keep than other butterflies, it is often found for sale in dealers' tanks on the east coast. It gets its name from the large ring spot near the base of its tail that looks like an eye.

The vagabond butterfly (*Chaetodon vagabundus*) is also easier to keep than most other butterflies. Its body color is lemon yellow with several attractive black stripes. It is found in the Pacific and Indian oceans.

The moon butterfly (*Chaetodon lunula*) is another easy-to-keep butterfly. Its colors are similar to the vagabond butterfly described above. It seems to be less timid in an aquarium than other butterflies. It is found in the same areas as the vagabond.

There are many other species of butterfly fishes that you may see in dealers' tanks. The chances are that most of them are very expensive and very delicate. You should only try to keep them after you have become very experienced in keeping other marine tropicals.

TANGS OR SURGEONFISHES

These fishes have sharp spines on each side of their bodies just in front of the tail. The spines can be extended or folded flat into grooves in the body surface of the fishes. You must be careful because the spines are very sharp. Tangs are algae eaters. (See page 41.) They should be fed plant material such as lettuce or spinach if there is not enough algae growing in the tank.

Tangs need lots of swimming room in the aquarium. If the tank is a large one they seem to do fairly well. Some of the tangs you may find for sale are the wedge-tailed blue tang (*Paracanthurus hepatus*) the sail-fin tang (*Zebrasoma veliferum*), the powder blue surgeonfish (*Acanthurus leucosternon*), and the lipstick surgeonfish (*Acanthurus glaucopareius*). All of these come from the Red Sea, or the Indian and Pacific oceans.

WRASSES

There is often a great difference between the color and pattern of a young wrasse and that of its parents. Sometimes the difference is so great that it is difficult to recognize that they belong to the same species. Males and females are also sometimes differently colored.

Wrasses are fairly hardy fishes for an aquarium and would make a good choice except for one drawback: at night and sometimes during the day many wrasses bury themselves in the gravel at the bottom of the tank. It is impossible to see where they are buried. You may not catch sight of them for several days. In order to find out if they are alive, you have to go through all the gravel to stir them up. Despite this drawback wrasses are peaceful fishes and good members of a community tank.

The clown wrasse (*Coris gaimard*) changes in an incredible manner as it matures. A young clown wrasse is red in color with three black-edged white spots on its body. It has a black-edged white stripe on the front and sides of its head. As it grows older, it loses the white spots and its body color changes to brownish-violet. An adult looks like a completely different fish. A clown wrasse is a hardy fish and a good eater once it gets used to a new aquarium. It is found in the Indian Ocean.

The blue streak (*Labroides dimidiatus*) is a very slender, dark blue fish with a lighter blue band running along its back. It is called a cleaner because it removes tiny animals that live in the skins of other fishes. Stories are told that many fishes will line up at a "cleaning station" near a group of cleaner wrasses to get their services. Even larger fishes such as groupers seem not to harm the cleaner when it is at work on their bodies. In an aquarium the cleaner soon learns to eat regular food. Cleaner wrasses are found over a wide range of the Pacific and Indian oceans and the Red Sea.

The Spanish hogfish (*Bodianus rufus*) is a very hardy fish and easy to keep when it is younger. As an adult it will grow too large for most home aquariums. Its body color is orange with a large violet patch on its back. It is found in many places on both sides of the Atlantic Ocean. A very similar fish is the Cuban hogfish (*Bodianus pulchellus*).

Other wrasses that you may see in dealers' tanks are the bluehead (*Thalassoma bifasciatum*) and the rainbowfish (*Thalassoma lunare*). Both are very beautifully colored and fairly hardy fishes once established in an aquarium.

SEAHORSES

Seahorses look like horses (at least their heads and necks do). Of course they are really just bony fishes. They are often very popular animals among people who do not keep marine aquariums. But for an aquarium keeper they present a number of problems.

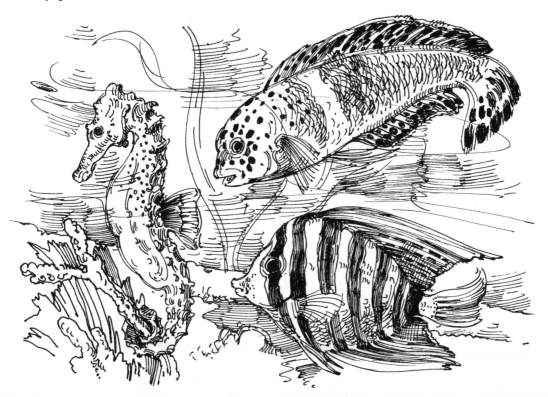

Seahorses cannot be kept with other fishes. A seahorse will attach itself to a piece of seaweed or a rock with its flexible tail. Then it will just stay there, eating only when a small food animal swims by. Because of its lack of movement, the sea horse can't compete for food with faster moving fishes.

Although a seahorse will eat only live food that moves past, you may be able to fool it into eating frozen brine shrimp. Keep the frozen shrimp in motion with a strong current of air from an air pump. The best foods for seahorses are live brine shrimp, daphnia (a freshwater relative of shrimp), and baby guppies.

Male seahorses have a pouch on their stomachs. A female sea horse will deposit fertilized eggs into the pouch. The eggs will hatch in the pouch and develop into perfect miniatures of the adults. When they are ready to come out, the male seems to be having convulsions. With every jerk of his body, he expels a bunch of tiny sea horses from his pouch. You may see this take place in your own aquarium. Separate the young from any adults quickly before they are eaten. Try to feed the young on newly hatched brine shrimp.

There are more than twenty-five different species of seahorses found all over the world. Some live in temperate waters and some live in tropical areas. Be sure you set up conditions that are best for the kind you may buy. Ask the dealer to make sure. Pipefishes, a somewhat similar looking species, breed in much the same way that seahorses do. Pipefishes are only rarely found in dealers' tanks.

OTHER FISHES

There are many other kinds of fishes that you may find for sale in a dealer's tanks. These include triggerfishes, filefishes, squirrelfishes, sweetlips, cardinalfishes, batfishes, parrot fishes, and moray eels. You may even find poisonous species such as lionfishes or turkeyfishes. Check carefully into any of these before you decide to buy. Ask the dealer and do some research on your own. The books listed on page 85 may help you.

·9·

Other Animals
for Your Aquarium

Fishes belong to a group of animals called vertebrates, animals that have a backbone. The animals in this chapter are all invertebrates, animals without a backbone. These include animals such as crabs, anemones, sea stars, and shrimps.

CRABS AND LOBSTERS

By far the best kind of invertebrate to keep in a marine aquarium is a hermit crab. Unlike most crabs which have a hard outer skeleton for protection, a hermit crab lives in an abandoned snail shell. When a hermit crab grows too large for its shell, it searches for a new, larger shell. If you keep a hermit crab in your aquarium, it's a good idea to supply a few empty shells for later use.

A hermit crab will scuttle across the bottom of the aquarium always on the lookout for food. If a fish comes too close, the hermit will raise its front claws in a threatening fashion. If the fish is persistent, the hermit may withdraw into its shell completely. Usually, however, a hermit crab will have little to do with the fishes in the aquarium.

Hermit crabs are good scavengers in an aquarium. They will pick up and eat any bit of leftover food they find. If you feed just enough for your fishes, try to provide a separate bit of food for the hermit crab in your tank.

Red hermit crabs (*Dardanus megistos*) from the waters around East Africa are often present in dealers' tanks. Sometimes you may find small anemones attached to their shells. When the hermit changes shells, it transfers the anemones to the new shell with its claws. Don't try to keep more than one hermit crab to a tank. They will fight with each other all the time.

Other kinds of crabs and lobsters should not be kept in the same aquarium as fishes. They will attack and eat anything that comes too close, including your prize fishes. Of course, you can try keeping them in a separate tank. Keep only small ones.

SHRIMPS

Two kinds of shrimps make fairly good members of a community aquarium. The banded coral shrimp (*Stenopus hispidus*) is red with white bands around its body and legs, and has long white antennas. Keep only one in a tank; they will fight with others of their kind.

Cleaner shrimps (*Hippolysmata grabhami*) are a deep red with a white stripe along their backs. They will groom some fishes, searching for small animals on their skins in much the same way as the cleaner wrasse. You can feed either species of shrimp on small bits of any animal food.

Both species can be kept in good health for several years in aquariums. Sometimes other kinds of shrimps are offered for sale in dealers' tanks. Check with the dealer carefully to see if they are safe to keep in your community tank.

ANEMONES

These many-tentacled animals look more like plants than animals. They are very sensitive to the water in newly set up tanks and should not be introduced until the tank is mature. They move (very slowly!) around the aquarium until they find a spot to their liking and settle down. This may take several days. At the bottom of an anemone's body is a foot disc which will stick to a flat surface such as a piece of rock or the side of the aquarium.

Keep only one kind of anemone in a tank because some kinds may be dangerous to others. In fact one anemone of any kind is enough for a community tank. Feed it a small bit of fish or shrimp flesh several times a week. Just drop the food into the tentacles and watch how it is devoured. If you forget to feed it, don't worry. Anemones can go without food for weeks, though it is not a good idea.

The anemones that live with clownfishes are the ones that are most often seen in dealers' tanks. These include ones from the genuses *Stoichactis*, *Radianthus*, and *Disco-*

soma. The *Stoichactus* are the hardiest. By the way, it is not uncommon for anemones to reproduce in a healthy aquarium.

OTHER INVERTEBRATES

Sea stars, octopuses, sea urchins, living coral, sea slugs, sea worms, and many other kinds of animals can be kept in marine aquariums. Almost all of these need special conditions and special care. They should not be kept in a community tank with fishes. They are very interesting animals however, and you might like to set up a special tank for some of them. Make sure that you ask your dealer and do research on your own about how to keep them. Some of the books and periodicals listed on page 85 will help.

·10·

Maintaining a Healthy Aquarium

There are many common-sense things that you can do to keep the fishes in your aquarium in good condition. Each day as you look in the tank you can easily observe all sorts of things. Here is a check list of some observations that you should get used to making almost automatically.

DAILY OBSERVATIONS

1. Check the thermometer to see if the temperature is in the right range. You can tell if the heater is working by watching to see if the indicator light is on.
2. Check to see that the lift tubes of the undergravel filter are bubbling.

3. Look to see how the fishes are behaving. Are any of them swimming in a peculiar manner? Are they rubbing themselves against the coral? (This may be an indication of a skin infection.) Are their colors bright and their eyes clear? If not, see the section on diseases later in this chapter.

4. After feeding, is all the uneaten food removed within five minutes? Do all the fishes get a chance at the food? Are you feeding the invertebrates correctly?

5. Are the lights working?

WEEKLY OBSERVATIONS AND CHORES

1. Check to see that the water level is maintained. It is a good idea to mark the level of the water on the outside of the tank with a small piece of tape or a crayon. Always use fresh water *not* saltwater to bring the water to the correct level. That's because water from the tank evaporates, but salt does not.

2. Check for the buildup of salt deposits on the outside of the aquarium and around the reflector. Wash off the salt with a clean sponge dipped in fresh water.

3. You may see some loose brown dirt on the gravel. This is called detritus. It may not be harmful, but it is unsightly. It can be removed by using a dip stick or by siphoning during a monthly water change. You can buy a dipstick or an easy-starting siphon at any aquarium dealer.

4. After the first few weeks, you will probably see algae growing on the coral and on the glass sides of the aquarium. Algae are not harmful to your fishes. Some of them may eat the algae. Some algae are also good for the water quality in the aquarium. But if too many algae grow on the front or the side glasses of the tank, it will cut down on what

you can see. The excess algae can easily be removed by a sponge. You can use a net to dip out any free-floating pieces that are not picked up by the sponge.

MONTHLY MAINTENANCE

1. The water should be partially changed every month. Siphon out about 10 to 20 percent of the water. (In a thirty-gallon tank, this would be from three to six gallons.) While you are siphoning try to remove any loose detritus on the bottom. Replace the water with newly made saltwater that is the same temperature and salinity as the water in the tank.

This will accomplish several things. First, the buildup of possible harmful chemicals in the tank is prevented. Second, the new saltwater contains trace elements that may have been used up by the fishes or the algae in the tank. Finally, changing water is a good way of getting rid of detritus and excess algae.

Note: do not change all of the water in the tank at one time. The strain on the fishes being moved into all-new water can easily kill them.

2. If you have an outside filter, it should be cleaned

every month. This can be done most easily by shutting off the air to the filter and removing it from the side of the tank. Rinse and scrub the filter to remove detritus and algae. Replace the filter fiber and *half* of the activated carbon. Replace the filter and start up the air again. Using all-new activated carbon will change the chemical content of the water too rapidly and be a shock to the fishes.

3. If you have to oil your pump or filter, do it now. Make sure you follow the instructions that came along with the unit. (Vibrator pumps do not need oiling.)

4. Dust the outside of the aquarium and wipe everything down with fresh water.

DISEASES

Velvet disease, or *Oodinium,* is about the most common disease found on marine fishes in an aquarium. It is caused by a protozoan, a microscopic animal, that attaches itself to the skin of a fish. Normally, the animal cannot be seen on the skin until the disease is well advanced and the fish quite sick. An infected fish loses its shiny appearance and looks as if it is covered by velvet. There are chemicals that can be used to cure the disease, but often they are given too late and the fish dies.

The best way to cure the disease is to prevent it

from breaking out. Keep the water in your aquarium of good quality and the fishes well fed. Healthy fishes can usually fight off the disease by themselves. If you must use a chemical cure, buy one ready mixed at your dealer. Be sure to follow exactly the instructions that are supplied.

White-spot disease, *Cryptocaryon,* is also caused by a microscopic protozoan that buries itself in a fish's skin. It is less dangerous but more difficult to cure than velvet disease. The treatment is the same for both.

Fungi and bacteria of all kinds may also attach to marine fishes. They may cause fin and body rot or spots on the body. It is best that the fishes that develop any of these diseases be promptly removed to a separate smaller tank and treated there. Describe what the disease looks like and ask your dealer for the medicine he recommends. Unfortunately, by the time you notice most of these diseases, the fish is usually too far gone for medicine to do much good.

Still other diseases may be caused by viruses, fish lice, or flatworms. Many of these are very difficult to cure. If you want to try, consult your aquarium dealer or one of the books for advanced aquarists listed on page 85.

Finally, don't be discouraged by all the diseases that your fishes may contract. The most dangerous time is when you are first setting up the tank. Once your tank is set up and working well, the chances are that a disease will not break out.

·11·
Hints
for the Beginner

There is no substitute for your own experience in keeping saltwater aquariums. You can read all the books and magazine articles that you can find and still not be as skillful an aquarium keeper as someone who has practical experience. That doesn't mean that you shouldn't find out all you can before you set up an aquarium. Find out what you can beforehand and then make changes in the light of your own experience. Here are some hints to help you; perhaps you can add to this list as you gain experience yourself.

• Collecting ocean water along many coastal areas is a risky business. The water may look clear after it has been filtered, but it may be teeming with bacteria and other microscopic life. You can usually make it safe for use in an aquarium by keeping it in the dark and aerating it for two weeks. Then shut off the air pump and allow the water to settle for several hours before you use it. Use a siphon to remove the water from the container. Discard the bottom inch of water left in the container. Placing a single inexpensive fish in the water will test it for use in an aquarium.

• Plastic aquarium decorations such as sunken ships, treasure chests, and divers are a matter of taste. My own opinion is that they look ridiculous. In an aquarium you are

trying to create a window to look into the world of nature. A plastic model looks out of place and ugly among natural coral rocks.

• Marine plants, other than the algae which grow naturally, are very difficult to maintain in an aquarium for a beginner. Without the correct water chemistry and the right amount of light, they will quickly die and pollute the water. You are probably better off not trying.

• Overcome the temptation to try to keep a big colorful angelfish or butterfly fish in a newly set-up aquarium. There is nothing more discouraging than seeing a prize fish die in a few days. There are many hardy fishes that are also quite colorful. Reread the chapter on beginner's fishes and choose one of those.

• Avoid buying gadgets such as ultraviolet radiation tubes or ozone generators. They can do more harm than good in unskilled hands. Equipment like that are definitely for use by advanced aquarists. On the other hand, the materials listed on page 22 are essential for success. Be sure to use them in setting up and maintaining your aquarium.

• Once your aquarium has been set up and is in operation for several months, everything will become much easier. The fishes will do much better in an established aquarium, even though it may not look as clean and spotless as a newly set-up tank. The algae growth on the back of the aquarium and on the coral is a sign that all is well with the water. If the algae stop growing, it may be time to replace 10 percent of the aged water in the tank with freshly made water.

· Don't use artificially colored coral in your aquarium. The dyes used to color the coral may not be chemically safe for fishes. Also avoid those corals that are very thin and easily breakable. Coral purchased at a dealer has usually been bleached white. Make sure that you rinse it thoroughly before using it in your aquarium. Collected coral should first be bleached then rinsed according to the directions on pages 20–21.

· There are almost unlimited choices that you can make in setting up a community aquarium. Here are just a few suggestions that you can use or modify as you like. All the suggestions listed below could probably be increased by one or two fishes without any danger.

TWENTY-GALLON AQUARIUM

1. 2 clownfishes (any species)
    1 damsel (tri-mac or blue devil)
    2 neon gobies
    1 hermit crab
2. 3 clownfish (percula)
    2 anemones (Stoichactis, Discosoma, or Radianthus)
    1 hermit crab
3. 1 heniochus

      1 damsel

      1 angel (choose a hardy species)

      1 coral shrimp

4.   2 scats

      2 monos

      2 damsels (any species, but one of each)

      1 hermit crab

5.   1 grouper (any species)

      2 cleaner wrasses

      2 damsels (any species, but one of each)

      1 hermit crab

6.   4 gobies (any species)

      2 clownfishes

      1 hermit crab

THIRTY-GALLON AQUARIUM

1. Any combination of six to eight clownfishes

      1 or 2 anemones

      1 hermit crab

2.   2 wrasses (clown wrasse or Spanish hogfish)

      1 panther grouper

      2 damsels

      1 hermit crab (larger size)

3.   1 angelfish (hardy species)

      1 butterfly fish (hardy species)

      2 cleaner wrasses (Labroides)

      1 hermit crab

Of course you can keep more fishes in larger aquariums. But remember not to keep more than one fish of any species that will fight with others of its kind.

· Finally, the best advice for a beginner is to begin. You'll learn as you go along. Many of the things that seem to be so difficult when you read about them turn out to be much easier when you do them. In practically no time at all you'll be able to give good advice to your friends who are just beginning. Keeping marine tropicals is an enjoyable and interesting hobby. You just may become hooked on it for life.

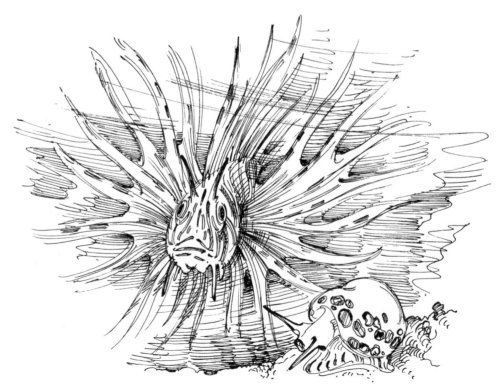

For Reading and Research

Axelrod, Herbert, and Vorderwinkler, William. *Saltwater Aquarium Fish*, Jersey City: TFH Publications, 1972.

Berrill, N. J. *The Life of the Ocean*. New York: McGraw-Hill, 1966.

Cox, Graham F. *Tropical Marine Aquaria*. New York: Grosset and Dunlap, 1972.

deGraaf, Frank, and van den Nieuwenhuizen, A. *Marine Aquarium Guide*, Harrison, New Jersey: The Pet Library Ltd., 1973 (more advanced).

Engel, L. *The Sea*. New York: Time-Life Books, 1961.

Herald, Earl S. *Living Fishes of the World*. New York: Doubleday, 1961 (more advanced).

Ommanney, F. D. *The Fishes*. New York: Time-Life Books, 1963.

Simon, Seymour. *From Shore to Ocean Floor*. New York: Franklin Watts, 1973.

Spotte, Stephen. *Fish and Invertebrate Culture*. New York: John Wiley & Sons, 1970 (more advanced).

Spotte, Stephen. *Marine Aquarium Keeping*. New York: John Wiley & Sons, 1973 (more advanced).

Straughan, Robert. *The Salt-Water Aquarium in the Home*. A. S. Barnes, 1969 (more advanced).

PERIODICALS

The Marine Aquarist
P.O. Box 35
Marlboro, Massachusetts 01752

Tropical Fish Hobbyist
T.F.H. Publications, Inc.
211 West Sylvania Avenue
Neptune City, New Jersey 07753

Index